T0368482

Balboa Press books may be ordered through booksellers or by contacting:

Balboa Press
A Division of Hay House
1663 Liberty Drive
Bloomington, IN 47403
www.balboapress.com
1 (877) 407-4847

ISBN: 978-1-5043-9364-5 (sc)
978-1-5043-9365-2 (e)

Library of Congress Control Number: 2017918901

Print information available on the last page.

Balboa Press rev. date: 01/25/2019

BALBOA
PRESS
A DIVISION OF HAY HOUSE

HOLLYWOOD DECO FASHIONS *of the* 1920s

The Art of Designing Fashions During Hollywood's Golden Age

by

Marianne Dunat

Compiled by

Roland J. Bain

[rjbain@att.net   916-922-3223]

TABLE OF CONTENTS

FOREWORD

During the early 1920s, Hollywood's motion picture industry was at the leading edge of its "golden age" when twenty-one-year-old Marianne Dunat arrived. Little did she know when she left her small, isolated village in the south of France in 1919 that her intended one-year stay would become an extended odyssey by her becoming a costume designer at a famous Hollywood movie studio.

The motion picture industry was gaining tremendous popularity with the public because of its newness and glamour. Such stars as Gloria Swanson, Clara Bow and Mary Pickford not only helped establish Hollywood's fame, but also helped create what became the indispensable costume-design department.

Budding movie studios were producing progressively more lavish extravaganzas with the accompanying demand by female stars for increasingly flamboyant costumes. Initially, stars furnished their own costumes; however, as the industry grew, productions expanded with the result that designers and seamstresses were hired to accommodate the burgeoning demand for sensational costumes. The costume-design department was born.

This, then, was the milieu in which Marianne Dunat became a part of Hollywood's film industry's "golden age" of the 1920s.

FROM A SMALL

FRENCH VILLAGE

TO

DESIGNING FASHIONS

DURING HOLLYWOOD'S

GOLDEN AGE OF MOVIES

– A 1920s' ODYSSY –

MARIANNE DUNAT'S ODYSSEY BEGINS

Marianne Dunat's odyssey began when she left her small village in the south of France and arrived in Hollywood in 1919. Shortly after her arrival, she found employment as a travel companion for the wife of a multi-millionaire. Occasional trips to New York and Paris allowed her to attend fashion shows with her employer in both cities. She became enamored with the world of fashion as she witnessed the parade of elegantly attired models. This led to a strong desire to learn as much as possible about designing apparel. With her employer's encouragement Marianne enrolled in Hollywood's famous Diogot & Wolfe School of Costume Design. Her ultimate goal was to become a costume designer at a Hollywood movie studio.

LEARNING THE ART OF FASHION DESIGN at HOLLYWOOD'S DIOGOT & WOLFE SCHOOL OF COSTUME DESIGN

THE FASHION-DESIGN LESSONS BEGIN

Initially, design school was not what Marianne expected, the expectation, rather her hope, had been that she would immediately start designing clothing of one sort or another along the lines of the fashions she had seen in New York and Paris. It was not to be. She would soon learn that designing costumes would come much later. Before she would reach that phase, she would learn an incredible amount of detail regarding the female anatomy. The learning pace was slow and measured. Feeling awkward and uncomfortable at first, she soon settled into this new milieu and its rigorous program. While not in school she would spend as much time as possible with her drawing studies.

Specific anatomical features to be closely studied ranged from face and body to the forms of eyes and fingers and, as well, to hair styles and complimenting attire for the head. Whether the face or body, they were divided into narrow components and analyzed in great detail. Of note is the detail given to drawing the hand, especially the fingers. As these skills progressed, advancing from the basic nude form to designing the attire for that form, saw Marianne's innate skills surface. Her confidence grew in cadence with the honing of her skills. Her talent was obvious.

Other important facets of the program studied in considerable detail included matching hair color with complimenting colors of apparel as well as other color harmonies. Long lists of compatible or incompatible color combinations or contrasts were compiled in order to achieve the most desirable blend of colors in the designs.

Marianne's productivity increased. She became a prolific and accomplished designer. At some point along the learning path, she chose — Liane — as her non de plume for her finished works.

[Note: The designs contained in this publication were selected from Marianne Dunat's collection of, "Fashion Designs of the 1920s" (Copyright 2009 by Roland J. Bain.]

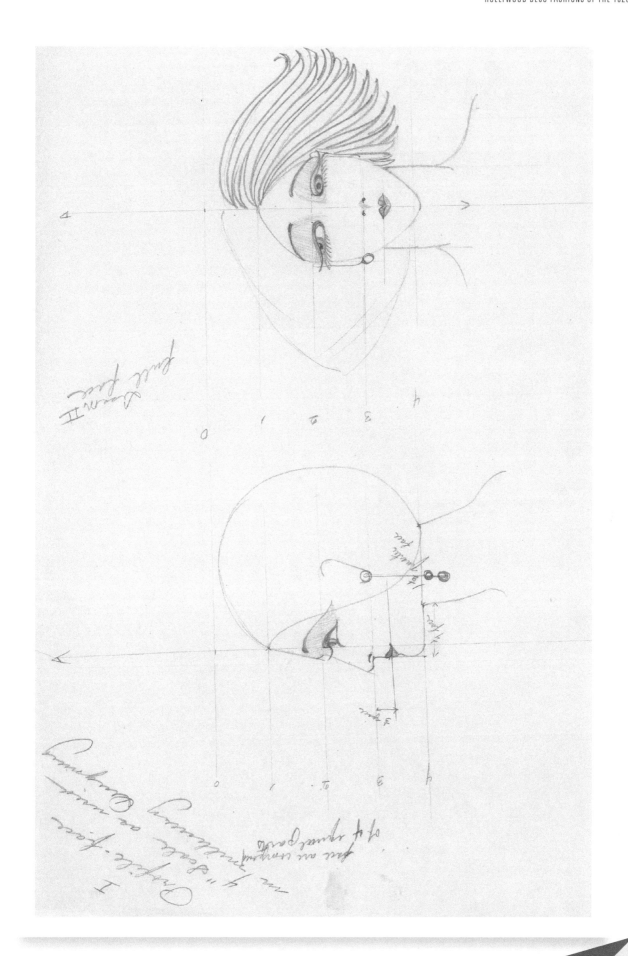

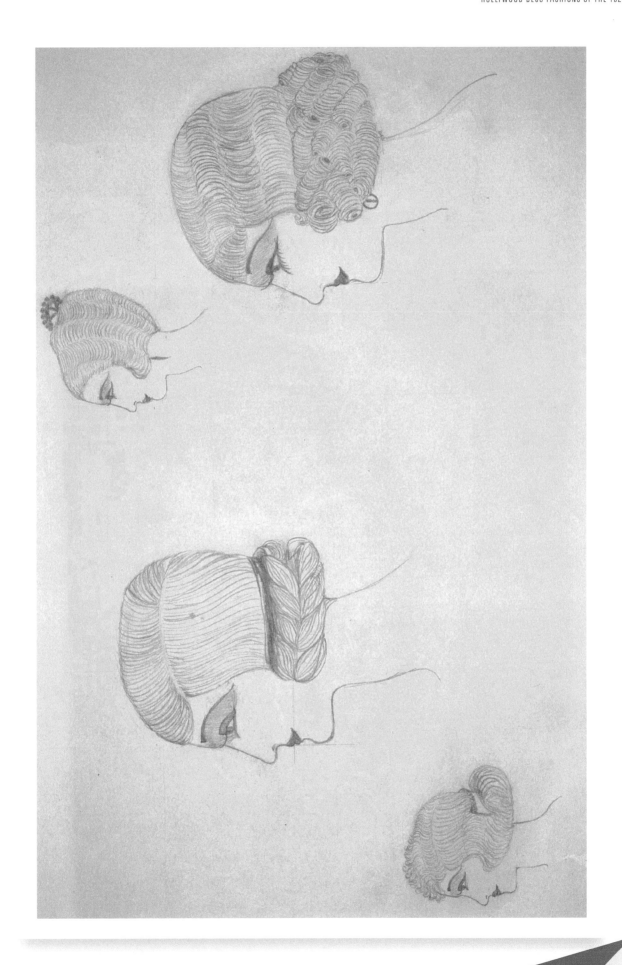

LEARNING TO PROPORTION THE ELEMENTS OF THE BODY AND THE RUDIMENTS OF THE ART OF FASHION DESIGN

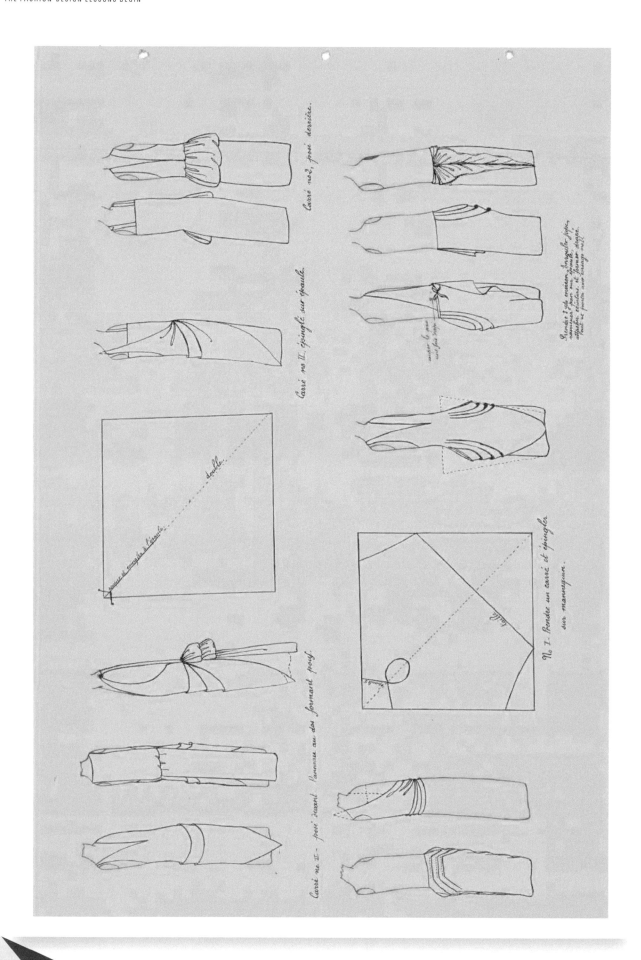

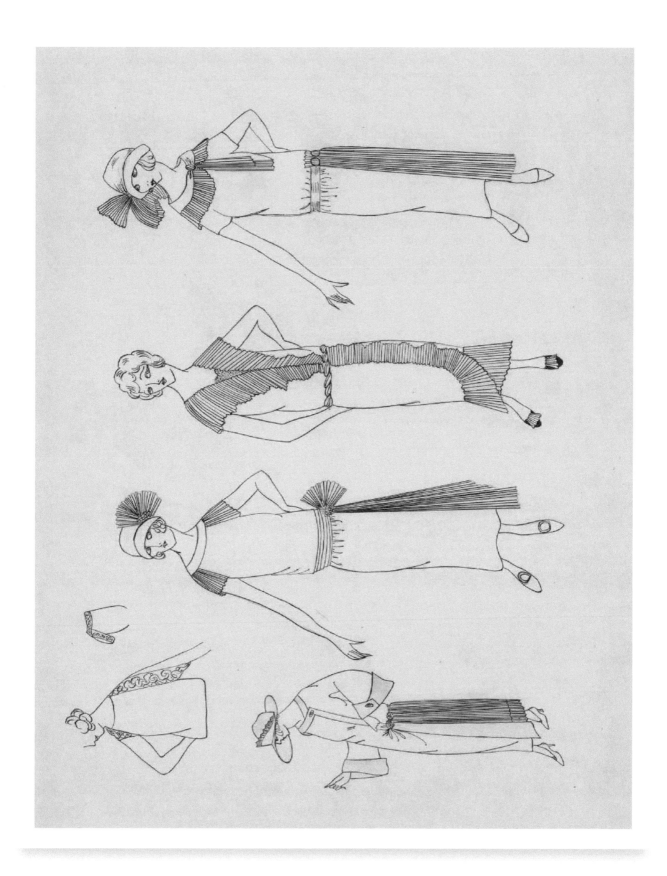

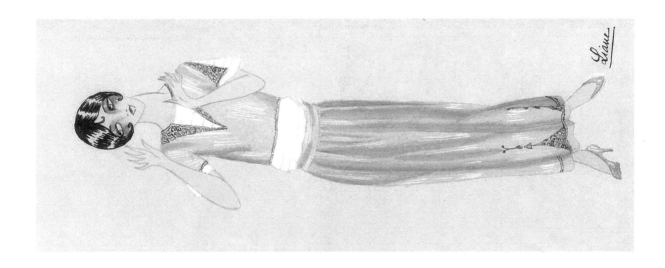

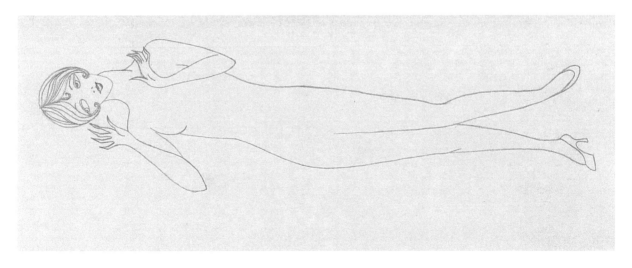

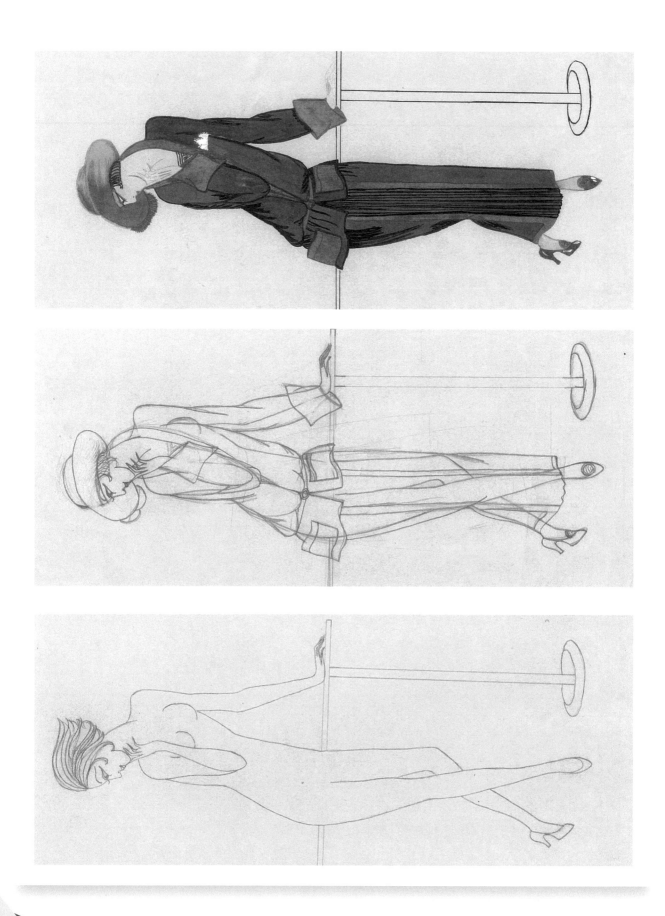

THE FASHION-DESIGN ARTISTRY
of Marianne Dunat "Liane"

DAY APPAREL

EVENING ATTIRE

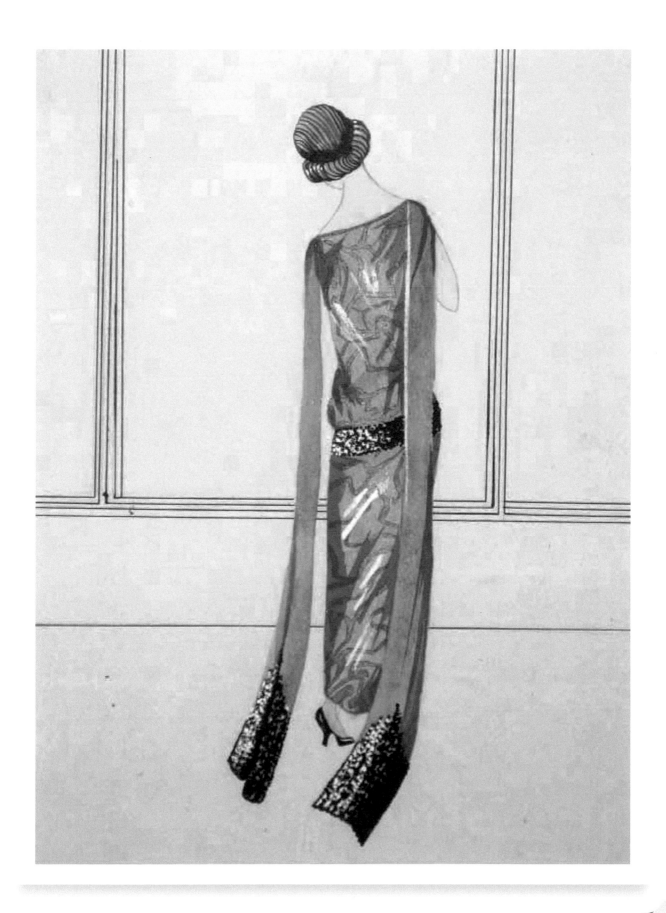

Liane

Liane

FURS

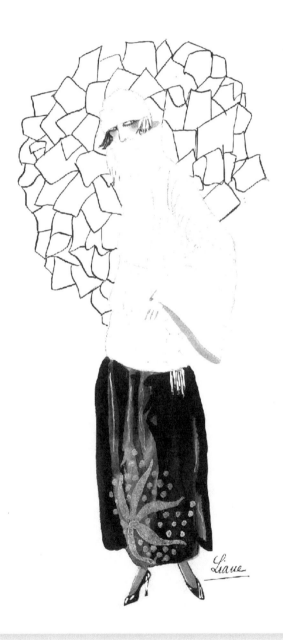

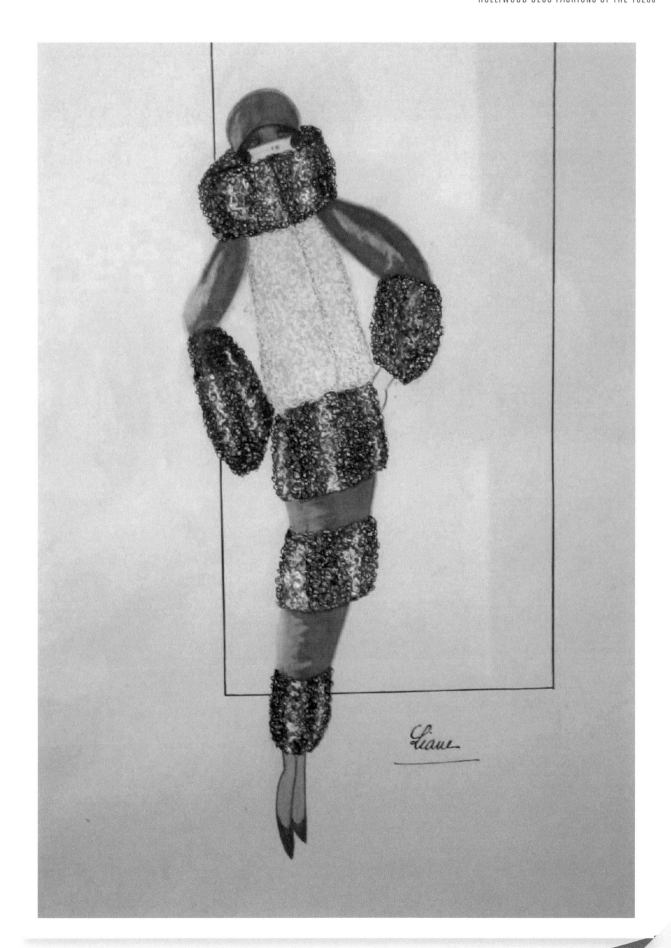

HARMONIES

COLOR

COLORS THAT MAY AND MAY NOT BE WORN BY VARIOUS TYPES OF WOMEN

FAIR BLONDE

Hair: flaxen, or golden. Eyes: Blue, brown or grey. Complexion: clear, little color.

BLACK-good, especially if of high luster and with touches of bright colors and white.

BROWN-good, especially very dark shades and green brown or bronze.

WHITE-good, especially clear or oyster white.

BLUE-all shades, if not too brilliant, including turquoise and peacock.

GREEN- good, both light and dark.

GREY- good, especially pearl, dove, and warm shades.

PURPLE- good, especially heliotrope, wisteria and blue-violet.

RED- Dark and brilliant shades like golf red are best.

YELLOW- avoid all yellow, except very pale yellow.

PINK- good, all delicate or subdued shades from lightest to old rose.

TITIAN BLONDE

Hair: Red, Eyes: Blue, grey or brown. Complexion: Medium, clear.

BLACK- good, especially transparent black.

WHITE- good, especially cream and ivory.

BROWN- rich, deep, dark brown is all right: avoid tan and yellow browns.

BLUE- good, especially blue-grey, midnight or darkest navy and sft, silent tones.

GREEN- use only darkest shades of pure color and bronze. Avoid light green Unless complexion is very clear and color good.

Grey- good, especially grey with a pink cast.

PURPLE- avoid if complexion is very clear and white. Lavender or violet may be used.

RED- Avoid.

YELLOW- Fair. Dark, rich orange or amber hues are best as trimmings or veiled by white or black.

PINK- lightest tints all right. Shell & flesh best.

BLONDE BRUNETTE OR IN-BETWEEN TYPE

Hair: light chestnut or brown tone. Eyes: hazel, grey, blue-grey or brown. Complexion: medium.

BLACK- fair, good if used with trimmings of color or white.

WHITE- good especially clear white or with pink tint.

BROWN- fair. Pinkish tan & golden brown are best.

BLUE- good, intensifies the color of blue-grey eyes; avoid very brilliant hues.

GREEN- fair, especially blue-green.

GREY- clear or blue-grey are fair. Avoid combinations of grey and black.

PURPLE- fair, darkest shades are best. Very clear complexion may wear lavender.

RED- good, in darkest shades, especially if used with very dark blue.

YELLOW- Palest yellow is fair. Avoid ecru tints.

PINK- good, especially pale pink and rose.

PALE BRUNETTE

Hair: Black or dark brown. Eyes: Brown, grey or blue. Complexion: Clear. Skin: fair, varying color.

BLACK- good, if white vest or color is used or if delicate color of soft material is used as trimmings.

WHITE- good, especially pure cream & ivory.

BROWN- fair, all shades.

BLUE- good, all shades, Electric & sapphire excellent if eyes are blue.

GREEN- only some shades of bronze, reseda, and bottle are good.

GREY- good, all shades, especially pearl, dove, blue-grey.

PURPLE- fair, must be used carefully; orchid is good.

YELLOW- Mustard, amber and canary yellow are best.

PINK- all pinks except where cheeks are highly colored.

OLIVE BRUNETTE

Hair: Dark brown or black. Eyes: clear, brown or black. Complexion: Dark in tone. Skin: smooth. Lips: deep red or purplish tinge.

BLACK- avoid.

WHITE- excellent, especially ivory and cream.

BROWN- fair, in very dark shades. Mahogany with cream for collar excellent.

Blue- excellent, if very dark.

GREEN- good in dark, silent tones.

GREY- fair, if warm color of grey.

PURPLE- use continuously, eggplant is permissible.

PINK- excellent in delicate tints. Salmon is especially good.

RED- excellent, especially the dark warm shades.

YELLOW- Terra-cotta or fawn shades are good if cautiously used. Apricot- in shear material or as trimming is excellent.

FLORIDE BRUNETTE

Hair: Black or dark brown. Eyes: Black, brown or grey. Complexion: dark. Skin: highly colored.

BLACK- very good especially with color touches & yokes of cream or ecru lace.

WHITE- good, especially cream and ivory.

BROWN- good, especially golden, tan and nut browns.

BLUE- very pale, dark or peacock; devoid of purple tinge is best.

GREEN- dark green is best.

GREY- silver grey is best. PURPLE- avoid, not becoming.

Red- cardinal, crimson, and clear red are best.

Yellow- good, including any tone from orange to ivory.

PINK- coral, rose pale, old rose and flesh are best.

SALLOW MATURE WOMAN

Hair: Grey or white. Eyes: Brown, blue or grey. Complexion: Sallow without color.

BLACK- good only with white or cream and touch of bright colors.

WHITE- only cream and milk white are good.

BLUE- midnight and navy without any tinge of purple are good.

BROWN- avoid.

GREEN- avoid.

GREY- good when of a warm color of grey.

PURPLE- avoid except in dull tones and with white at neck. Some lilac may be used.

RED- avoid, except in dull, wine shades & with white at neck.

YELLOW- avoid.

PINK- only old rose is good.

COLOR HARMONIES

BLUE and orange, perfect harmony.

BLUE and gold (or gold color).

BLUE and straw color harmonise.

BLUE and salmon, agreeable harmony.

BLUE and crimson (cramoisy) imperfect.

BLUE and drab, harmonise.

BLUE and stone, harmonise.

BLUE and chestnut or chocolate, harmonise.

BLUE and brown, agreeable harmony.

BLUE and white, harmonise.

BLUE and scarlet and purple or lilac, harmonise.

BLUE and orange and green, harmonise.

BLUE and brown, crimson and gold (or yellow).

BLUE and orange, black and white harmonise.

BLUE and pink, a poor harmony.

BLUE and lilac, a weak harmony.

BLUE and crimson, imperfect harmony.

BLUE and fawn, a weak harmony.

BLUE and grey, a cold harmony.

BLUE and black, a dull harmony.

• •

BLACK and white, perfect harmony.

BLACK and gold (or gold color) a fine harmony.

BLACK and orange, a rich harmony.

BLACK and maize, harmonise.

BLACK and primrose,

BLACK and salmon,

BLACK and pink,

BLACK and scarlet

BLACK and cerise,

BLACK and yellow green,

BLACK and fawn, harmonise.

BLACK and slate, a subdued harmony,

BLACK and grey, a quiet harmony,

BLACK and citrin, a quiet harmony.

BLACK and olive, a dull harmony.

BLACK, scarlet and blue-green, harmonise.

BLACK, crimson and lemon color, harmonise.

BLACK, crimson and yellow-green, harmonise.

• •

WHITE and orange, harmonise.

WHITE and scarlet,

WHITE and cerise,

WHITE and pink,

WHITE and brown,

WHITE and red and blue, harmonise.

WHITE, scarlet and blue-green, harmonise.

VIOLET and gold, a perfect harmony

VIOLET and orange-yellow, a rich harmony

VIOLET and maize, a vivid harmony,

VIOLET and tones of itself harmonise.

• •

YELLOW and purple, a perfect harmony

YELLOW and blue harmonise

YELLOW and violet,

YELLOW and deep crimson,

YELLOW and chestnut harmonise

YELLOW and black, a pronounced harmony

YELLOW and lilac, a weak harmony

YELLOW and white, a weak harmonyu.

YELLOW, purple, scarlet and blue harmonise.

• •

GREEN and red, a perfect harmony

GREEN and scarlet harmonise

GREEN and russet harmonise

GREEN and black, a dull harmony

GREEN, scarlet and blue harmonise.

GREEN (deep) and gold harmonise

GREEN, crimson, blue and gold harmonise

• •

ORANGE and blue, a perfect harmony

ORANGE and olive, harmonise

ORANGE and violet,

ORANGE and chestnut,

ORANGE and deep brown,

ORANGE, crimson and green,

ORANGE, crimson and blue,

ORANGE, purple and scarlet,

ORANGE, blue, scarlet and green,

ORANGE, violet, scarlet, white and green harmonise

PURPLE and yellow, a perfect harmony

PURPLE and gold, a rich harmony

PURPLE and maize harmonise

PURPLE and tones of itself harmonise

PURPLE and black, a heavy harmony

PURPLE and white, a cold harmony

PURPLE, scarlet and gold harmonise

PURPLE, scarlet and white,

PURPLE, scarlet, blue and orange,

SCARLET and blue-green harmonise

SCARLET and blue,

SCARLET and purple or lilac,

SCARLET and violet,

SCARLET, blue and white,

SCARLET, blue and grey,

SCARLET and slate,

SCARLET, blue, black, and yellow harmonise.

RED and green, a perfect harmony.

RED and gold, a bright harmony.

RED and grey, harmonise.

RED and white, harmonise.

RED and blue, a dull harmony.

LILAC and deep gold harmonise.

LILAC and primrose,

LILAC and maize,

LILAC and crimson,

LILAC crimson and gold,

LILAC and grey, a weak harmony.

LILAC and white, a cold harmony.

LILAC and black, a dull harmony.

MARIANNE FINDS HER PLACE IN HOLLYWOOD'S MOVIE INDUSTRY DURING ITS 1920S' GOLDEN AGE

MARIANNE'S PATH TO THE GOLDEN AGE OF MOVIES

In time, Marianne's portfolio of fashion designs took on imposing dimensions. The impressiveness and scope of her portfolio and a fortuitous meeting with one of Hollywood's leading costume designers (Claire West, future inductee into Hollywood's Costume Designer's Hall of Fame) served as Marianne's introduction to Hollywood's movie industry. Marianne's imposing portfolio led to her being invited to join Claire West's staff at the Cecil B. DeMille studios.

The opening chapter of her new career was memorable. She was one of a small cadre of designers/seamstresses working in very cramped quarters. One of her co-workers was Edith Head who, at the time had to be taught to be a "sketcher", and who later became Hollywood's premier costume designer.

Marianne's introduction to Hollywood films was DeMille's extravaganza, "The Ten Commandments". Her work consisted primarily of sketching designs. Because she was an excellent seamstress, she also helped craft the costumes.

Claire West had the reputation of being a taskmaster, a person very difficult with whom to work. Her eventual decision to leave the studio came as somewhat of a disappointment to Marianne given that she had learned quite a bit from her mentor. Claire was leaving in order to head the costume-design department at the new First National Studios. Her asking Marianne to accompany her at the new studio was a strong endorsement of Marianne's skills and talent as a costume designer. Very regretfully, Marianne declined. Thanks to the offer, along with the self-confidence she had achieved, Marianne Dunat felt that she had achieved her goal of becoming an acknowledged costume designer.

RETIREMENT

RETIREMENT

Marianne's marriage, coupled with raising two children, led to her retiring from the world of costume-design in the glamorous movie industry. She did continue creating designs, partly out of habit and for personal satisfaction, and partly as a favor for friends. She often pondered the point of what her life would have had in store for her had she stayed in her Basque village of Urepel. She couldn't conceive of anything that could have compared with the amazing adventures she had experienced. Certainly, the unique travel experiences, her having had the opportunity to develop her artistic skills, and her association with the exciting movie industry during its Golden Age would remain in that very special niche in her memory.

For years, much of her "retirement" was devoted to charitable endeavors for the French community in the greater Los Angeles area. She worked closely with the French Consulate in assisting needy people of French descent. For her untiring efforts, the French government awarded her the "L'Ordre National Du Merite." (The National Order of Merit).

Marianne Dunate Bain, the young lady from a small Basque village in the south of France who became a movie-studio costume designer during Hollywood's 1920s' Golden Age, passed away in December of 1998, one month after her 100th birthday. The President of France sent a personal note of condolence to her family.

Liane

ABOUT THE AUTHOR

Marianne Dunat's early life was not a simple one. Her family lived in a small village near the Spanish border where her very strict father worked as a Customs Officer. Her mother passed away when Marianne was 10, leaving her and her sister to manage the home, their father absent a good deal of the time. During her teen years she was sent to several of her relatives' homes in different near-by villages to learn general housekeeping: to cook, sew, and iron.

In 1919, at age 21, she was given the opportunity to visit relatives in Los Angeles for a year. The trip was not an easy one and it was a long one, it having taken an entire month for Marianne and her friend to reach Los Angeles.

Entering New York harbor after a ten-day crossing was an emotional one for Marianne. She had seen pictures of the Statute of Liberty, but that didn't compare with actually seeing — the "grand Lady". Then going through customs at Ellis Island was a lengthy and tiring process. One of the documents she had to have with her in order to enter the United States was a document with the title of…"Certificat de Bonnes Vie et Moeurs" (Certificate of Good Life and Morals).

> [Note: Ellis Island had been closed for decades. It re-opened in the early 1990s. Marianne's certificate is prominently displayed in a showcase in the —" Treasures From Home" wing at Ellis Island. Also, prior to the re-opening, an interview by an Ellis Island representative was taped for the purpose of having her experiences in coming to America recorded and preserved in the Oral history section. In addition, her name is inscribed on the Wall of Honor in the courtyard.]

The four-day train trip to Los Angeles took Marianne and friend through Indian country in New Mexico. The native Indians she saw at train stops frightened her, this experience not to be forgotten. Arriving in Los Angeles she learned that her relatives had moved to New Mexico. Because of her recent experience Marianne would not return to the Indian Country. Further, she was reluctant to return to small-village life. Her visit to the United States would go well beyond the intended one-year stay.

With the assistance of the manager at the boarding house at which she rented a room, Marianne found employment as a travel companion for the wife of a multi-millionaire. The die was cast, Marianne Dunat would become a permanent resident, a neutralized citizen, of the United States of America.

Printed in the United States
By Bookmasters